PIANO SOLO

CHRISTMAS CLASSIC
FAVORITES

D0504049

ISBN 978-1-4234-9477-5

HAL•LEONARD®
CORPORATION
7777 W. BLUEMOUND RD. P.O. BOX 13819 MILWAUKEE, WI 53213

Visit Hal Leonard Online at
www.halleonard.com

CHRISTMAS TIME IS HERE

from A CHARLIE BROWN CHRISTMAS

Words by LEE MENDELSON
Music by VINCE GUARALDI

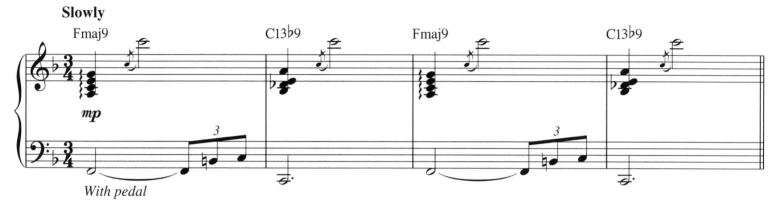

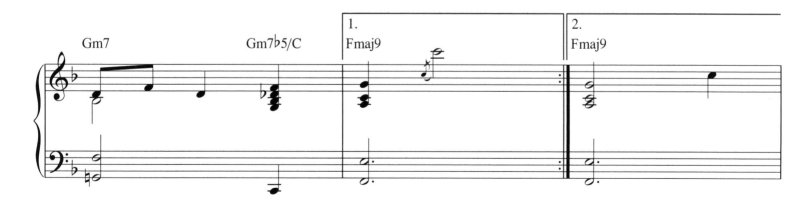

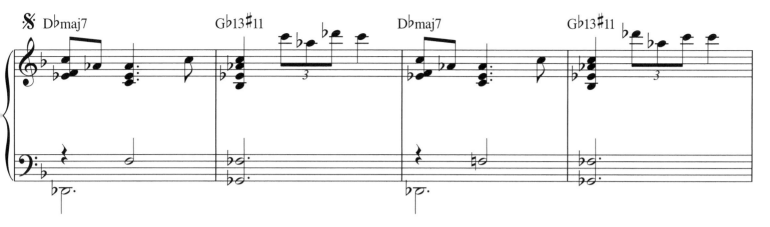

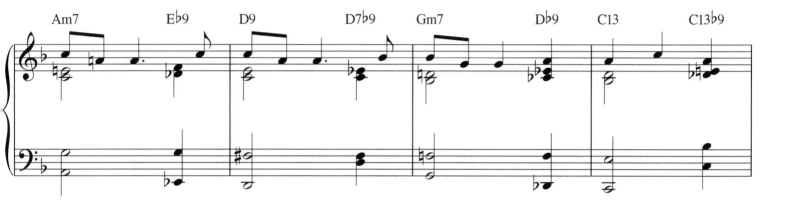

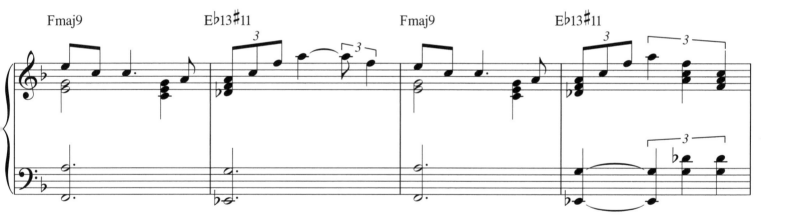

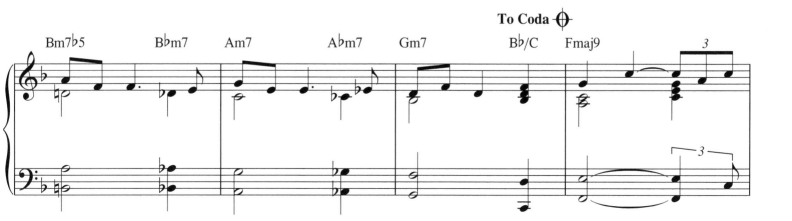

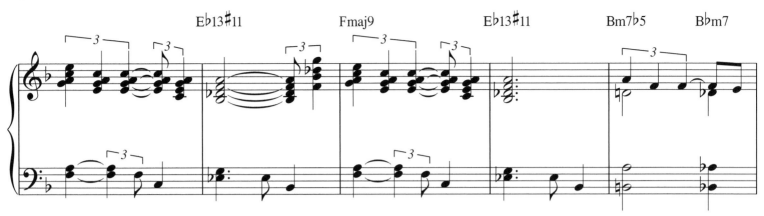

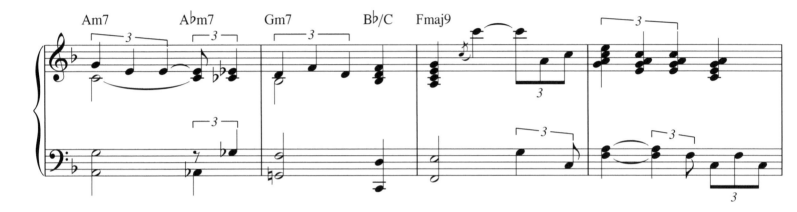

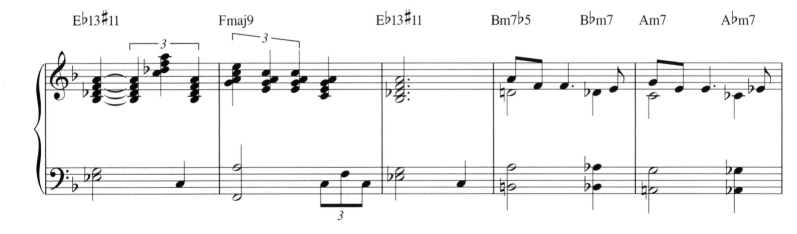

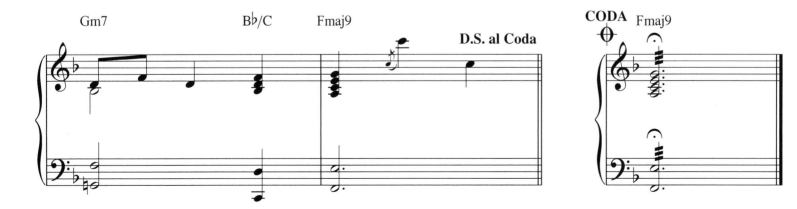

FROSTY THE SNOW MAN

Words and Music by STEVE NELSON
and JACK ROLLINS

Moderate Swing

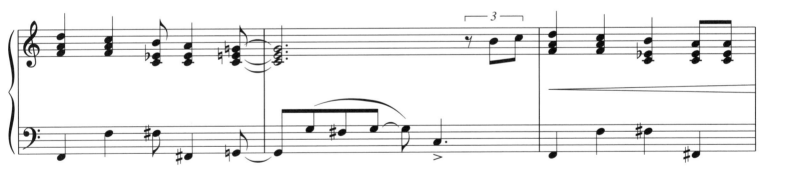

To Coda $\oplus$

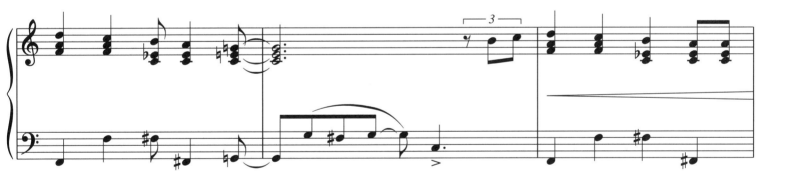

D.S. al Coda

CODA

Slowly, freely

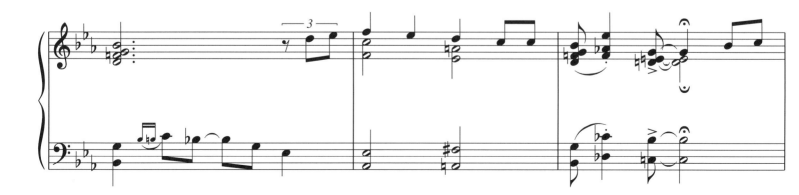

Tempo I

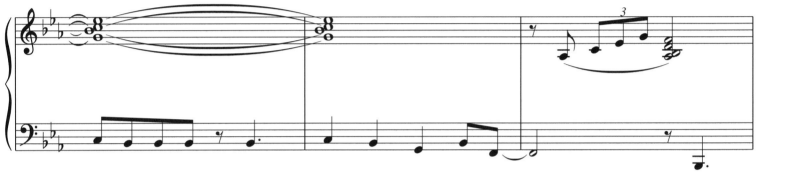

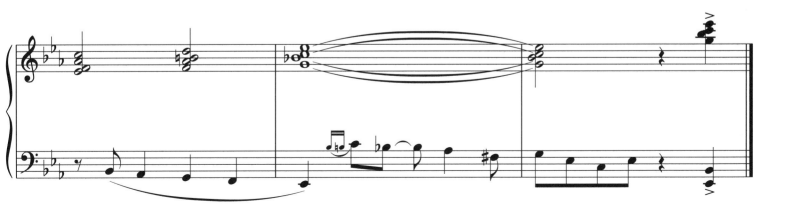

CHRISTMAS IS A-COMIN'
(May God Bless You)

Words and Music by
FRANK LUTHER

Moderately

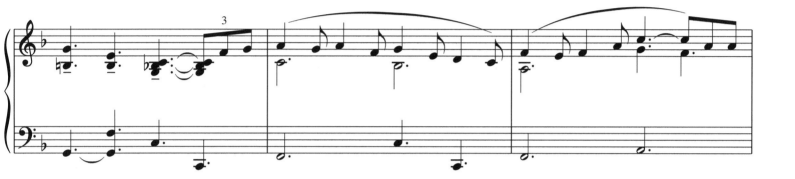

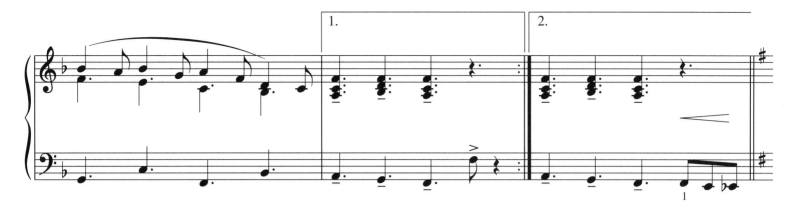

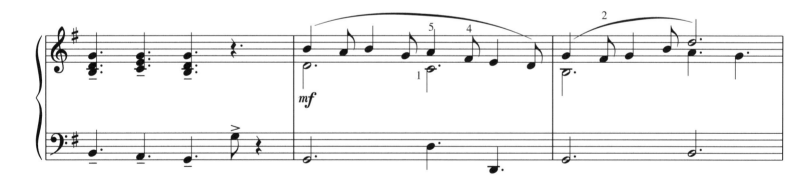

FELIZ NAVIDAD

Music and Lyrics by
JOSÉ FELICIANO

Moderately

HERE COMES SANTA CLAUS
(Right Down Santa Claus Lane)

Words and Music by GENE AUTRY
and OAKLEY HALDEMAN

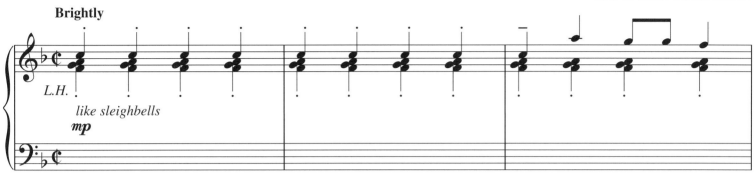

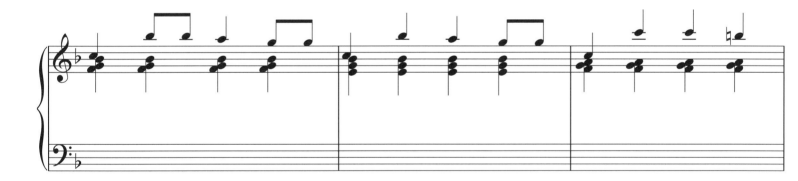

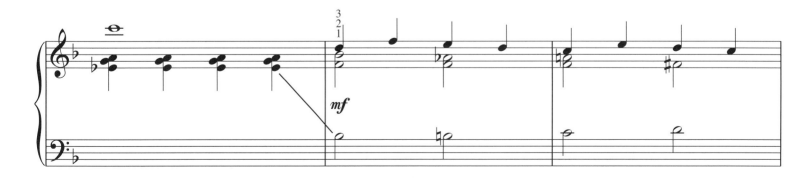

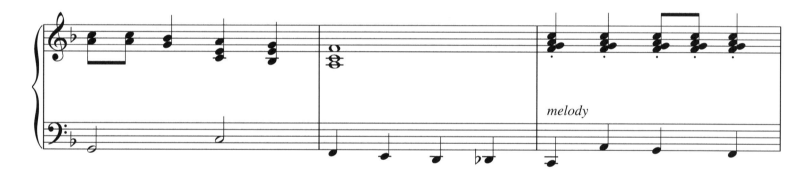

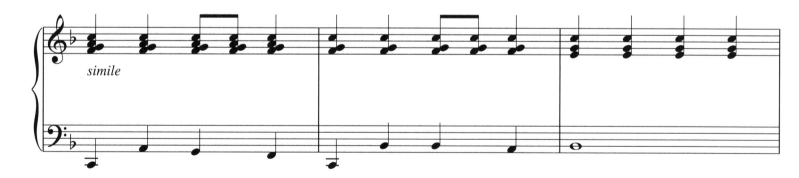

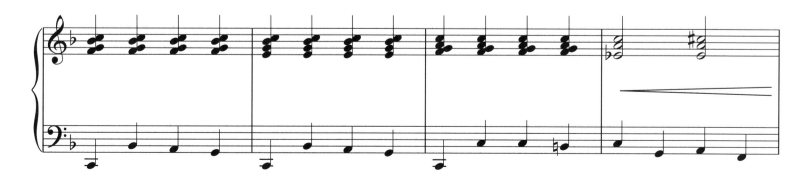

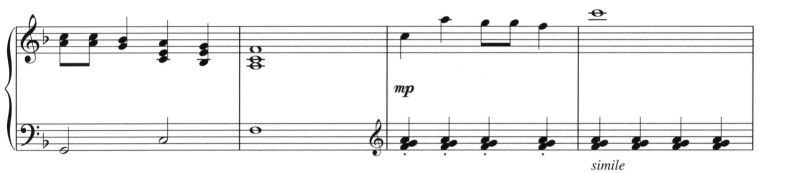

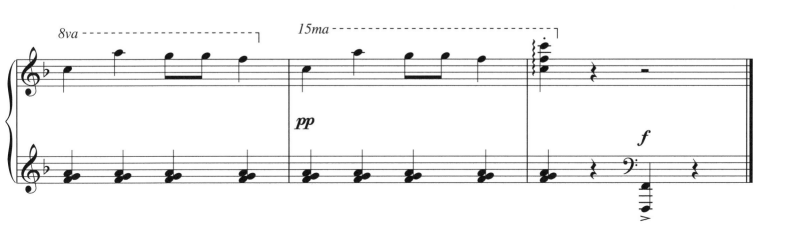

A HOLLY JOLLY CHRISTMAS

Music and Lyrics by
JOHNNY MARKS

Moderate Swing

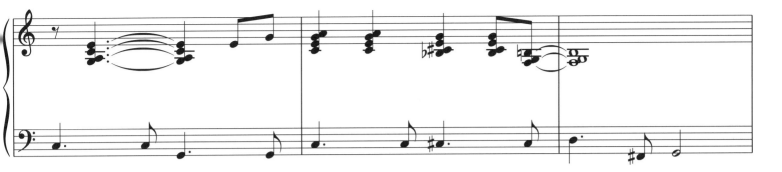

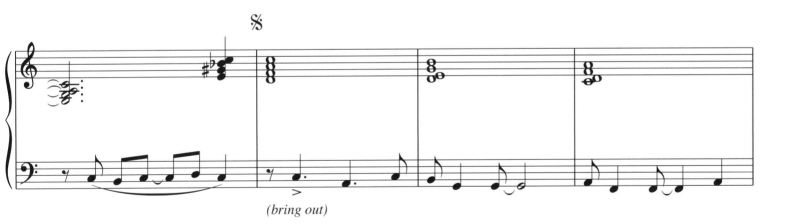

(bring out)

To Coda ⊕

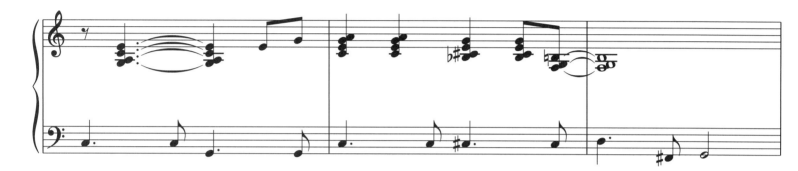

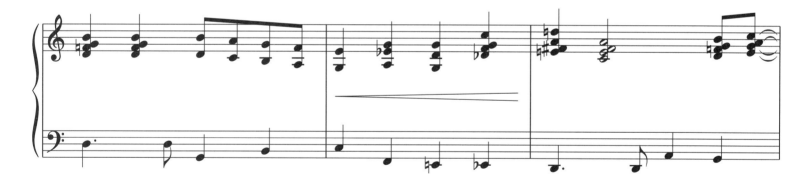

1.   2.   **D.S. al Coda**   **CODA**
⊕

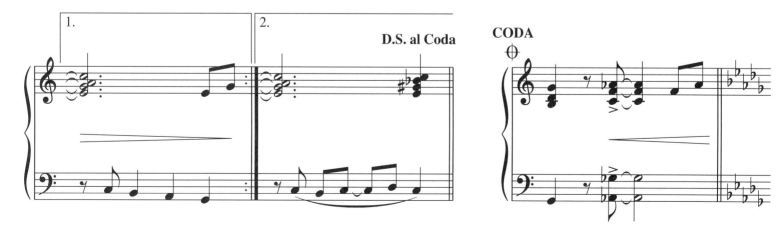

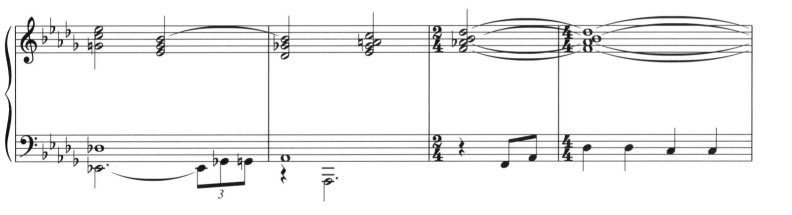

(There's No Place Like)
HOME FOR THE HOLIDAYS

Words by AL STILLMAN
Music by ROBERT ALLEN

Moderately (somewhat rubato)

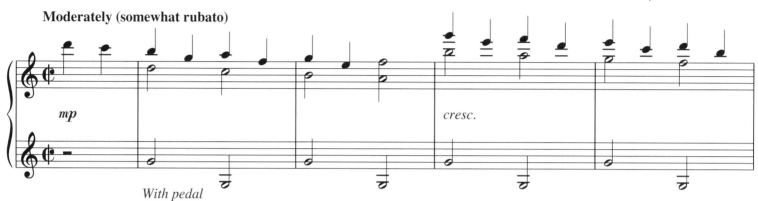

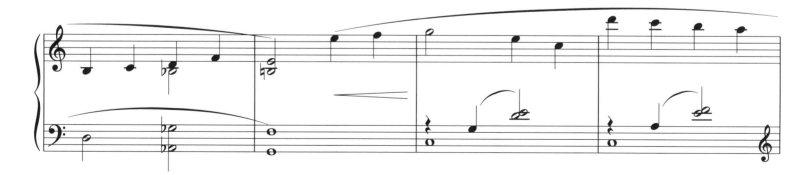

Medium bright Country

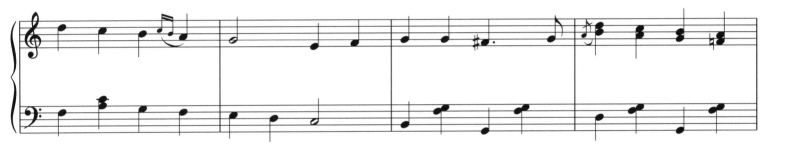

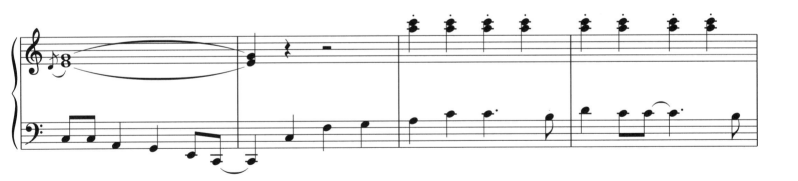

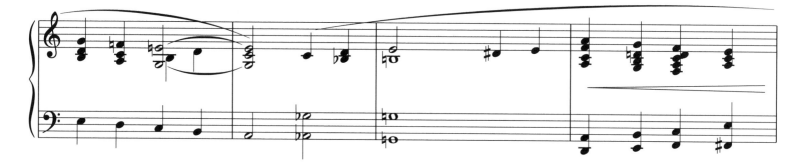

A MARSHMALLOW WORLD

Words by CARL SIGMAN
Music by PETER DE ROSE

Brightly

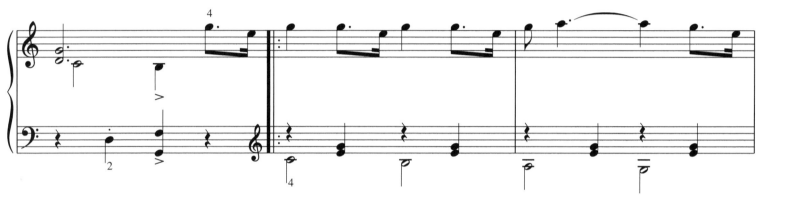

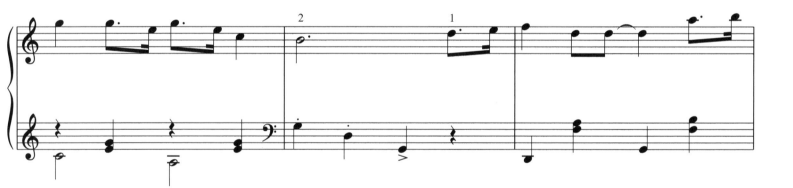

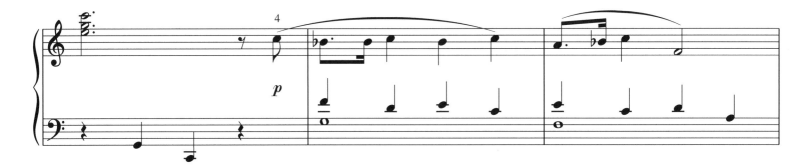

cresc.

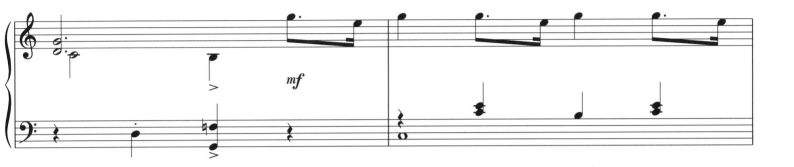

mf

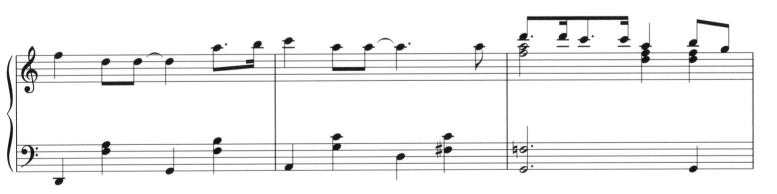

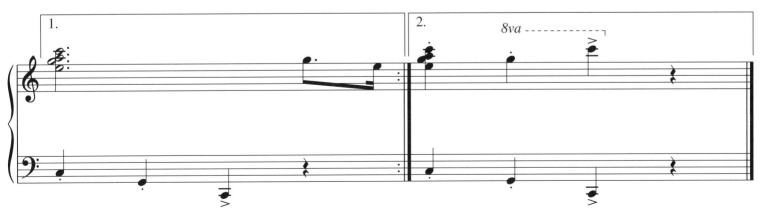

1.

2.

8va - - - - - - - - - - - -

LITTLE SAINT NICK

Words and Music by BRIAN WILSON
and MIKE LOVE

Moderately fast Rock 'n' Roll

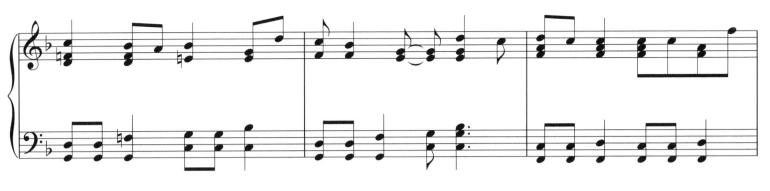

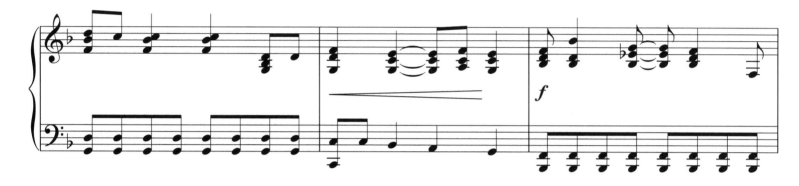

MISTLETOE AND HOLLY

Words and Music by FRANK SINATRA,
DOK STANFORD and HENRY W. SANICOLA

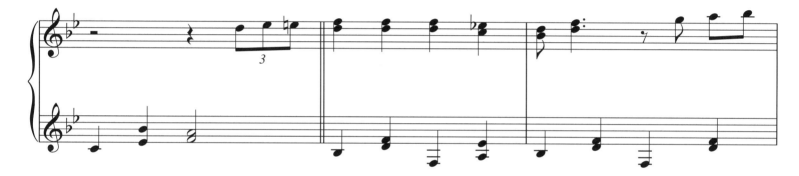

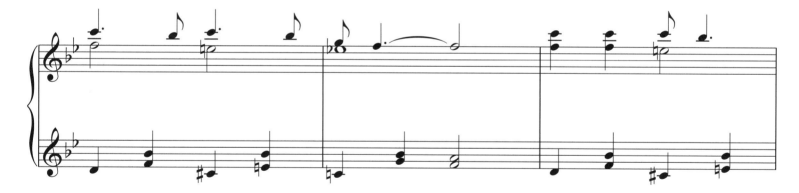

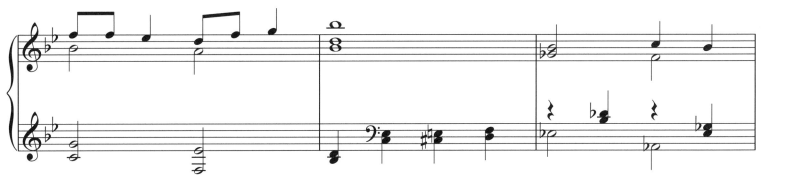

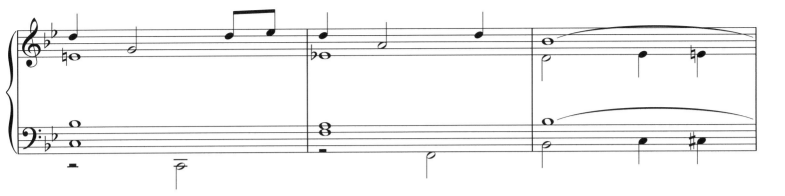

THE MOST WONDERFUL TIME OF THE YEAR

Words and Music by EDDIE POLA
and GEORGE WYLE

Bright Waltz

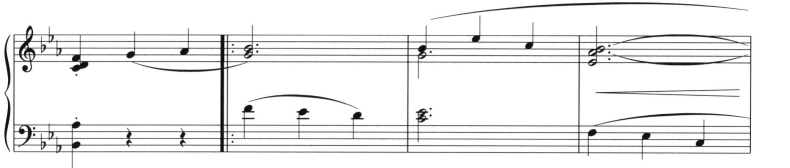

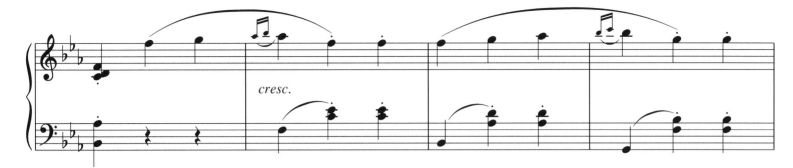

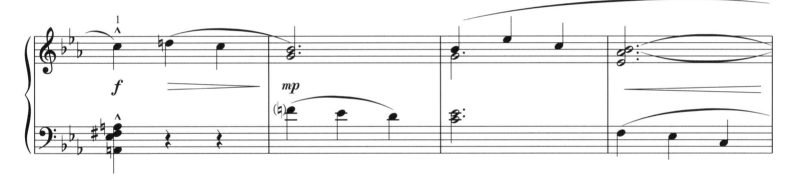

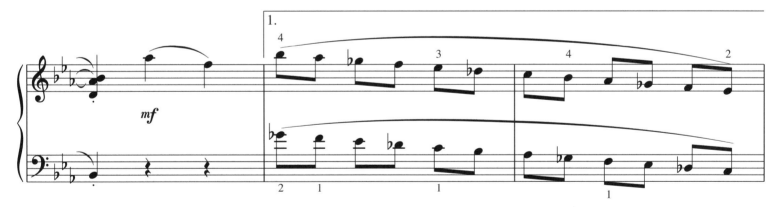

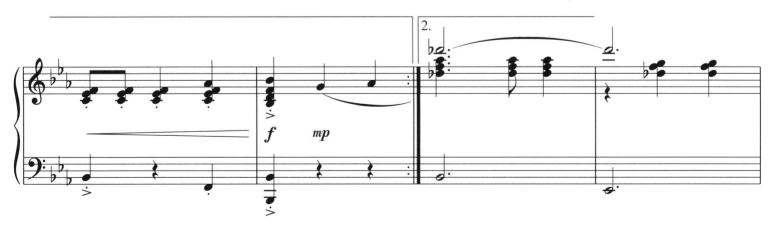

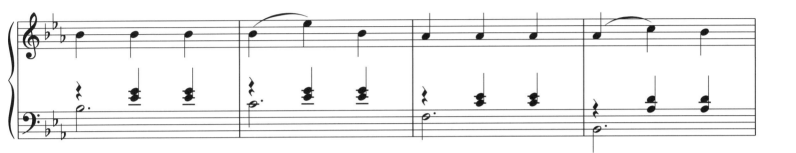

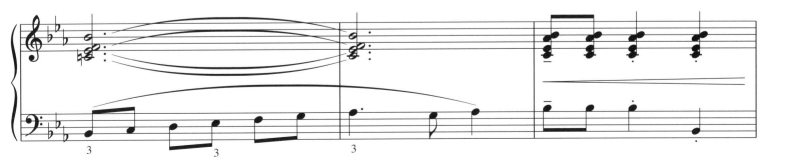

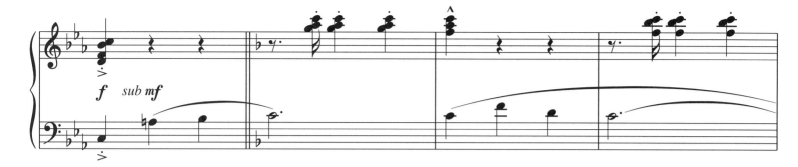

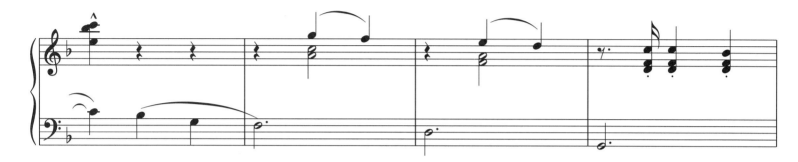

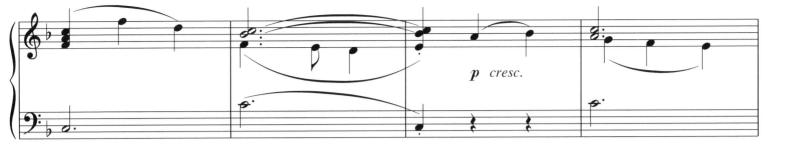

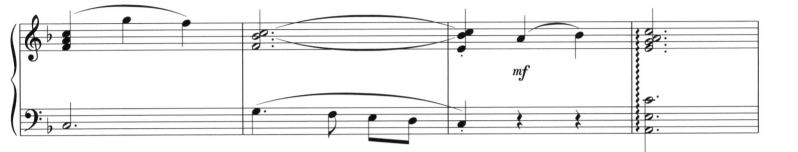

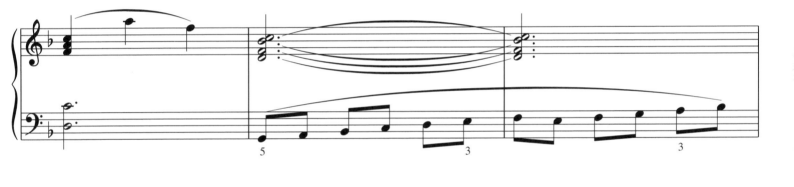

NUTTIN' FOR CHRISTMAS

Words and Music by ROY BENNETT
and SID TEPPER

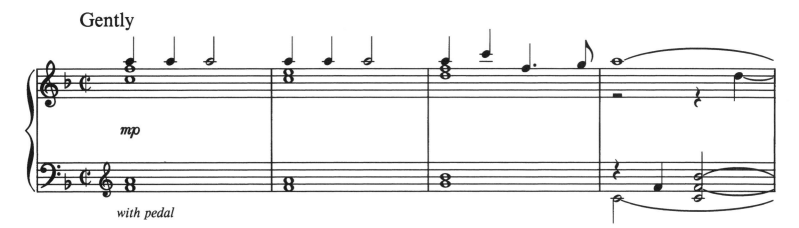

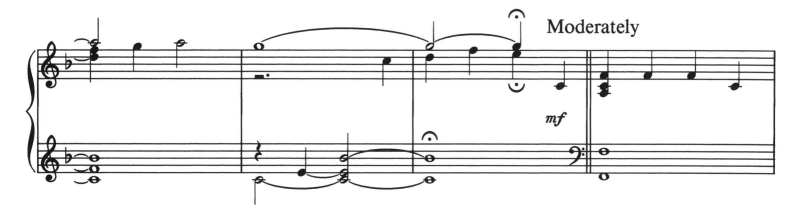

Brightly, not too fast

48

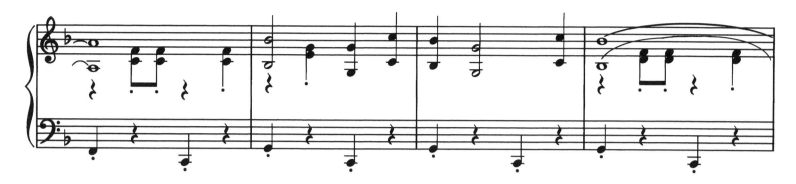

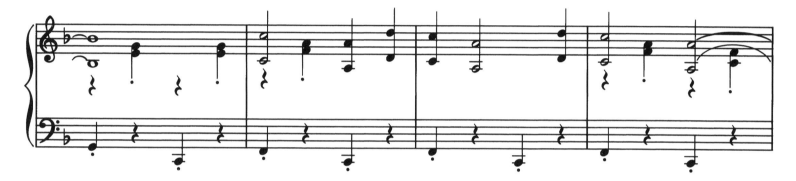

pedal

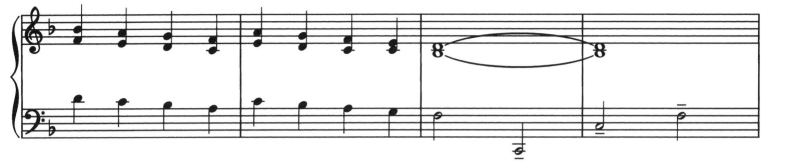

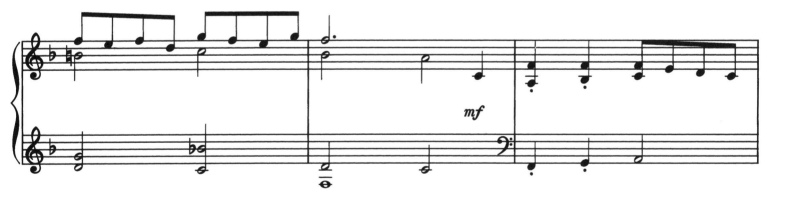

pedal

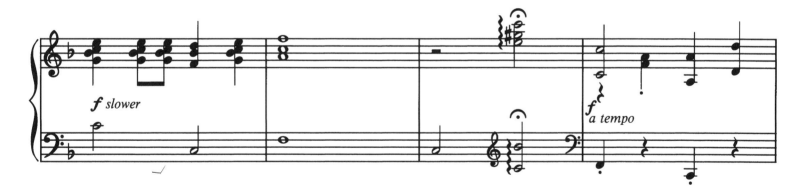

f slower

f a tempo

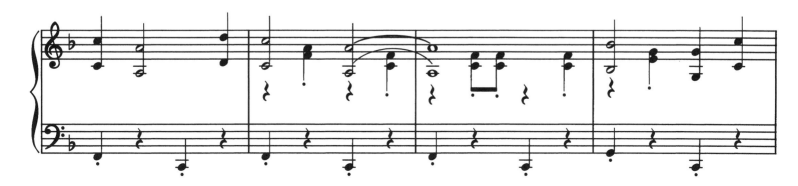

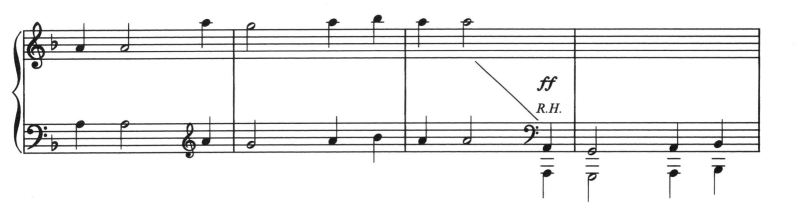

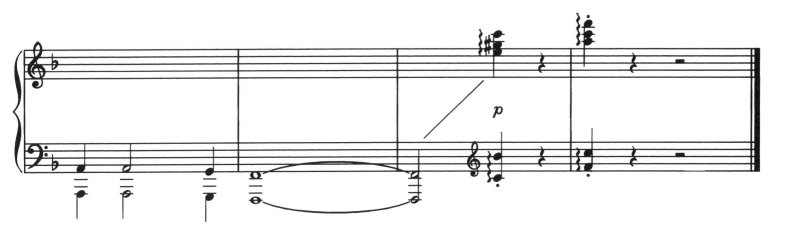

OLD TOY TRAINS

Words and Music by
ROGER MILLER

With a steady beat

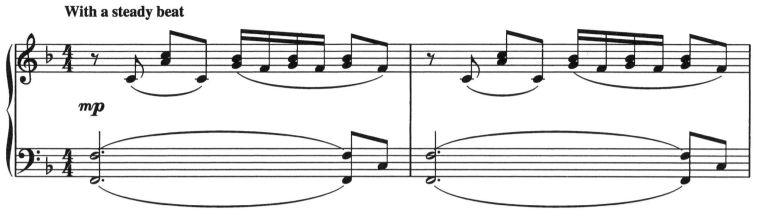

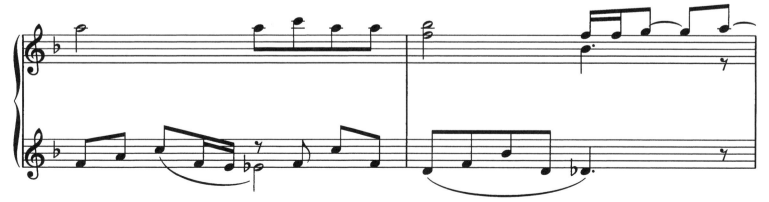

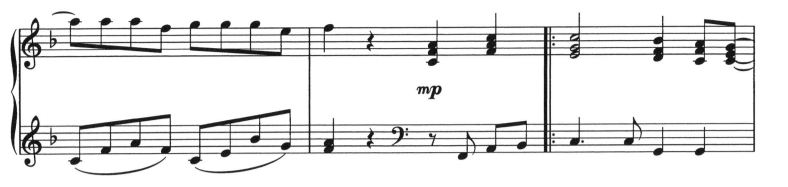

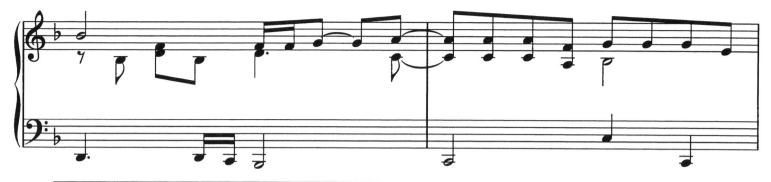

1.

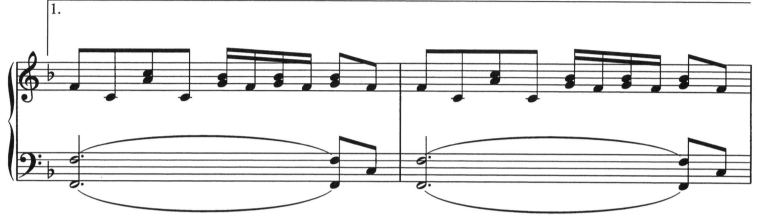

2.

slowly

a tempo   *rit.*

SNOWFALL

Lyrics by RUTH THORNHILL
Music by CLAUDE THORNHILL

Moderately slow

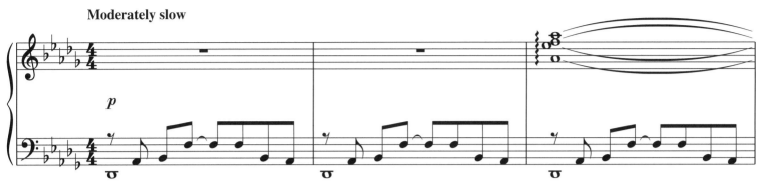

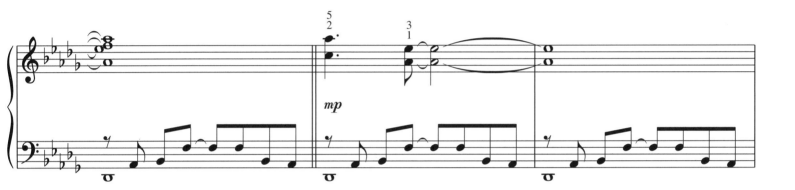

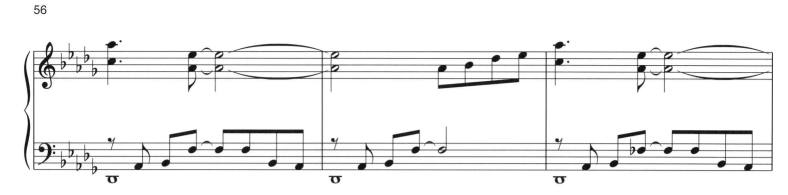

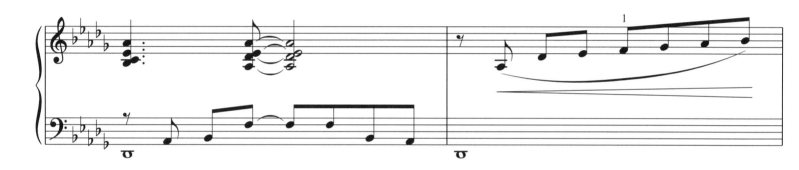

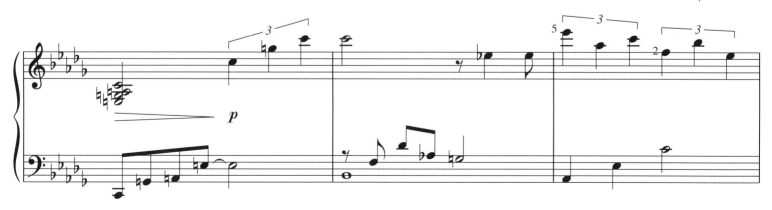

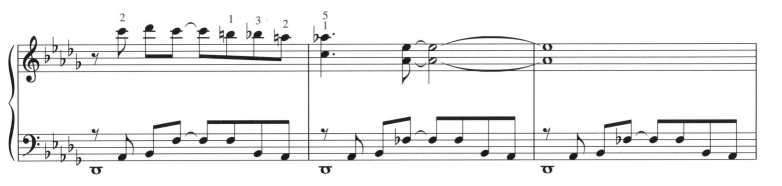

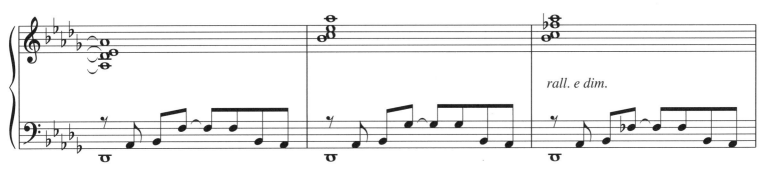

PRETTY PAPER

Words and Music by
WILLIE NELSON

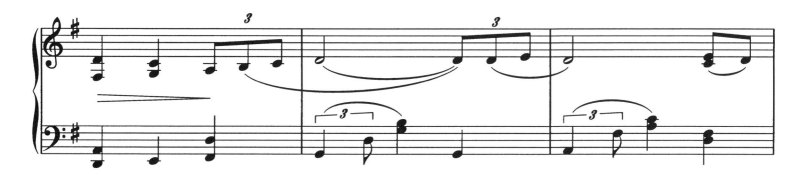

ROCKIN' AROUND THE CHRISTMAS TREE

Music and Lyrics by
JOHNNY MARKS

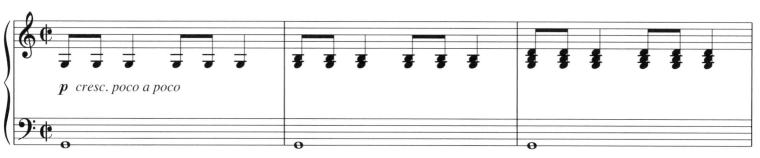

(bring out)

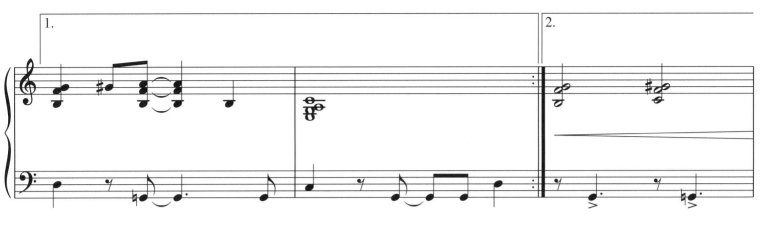

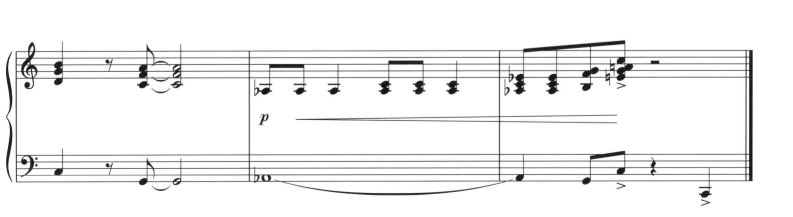

SANTA CLAUS IS COMIN' TO TOWN

Words by HAVEN GILLESPIE
Music by J. FRED COOTS

Light, sophisticated Swing

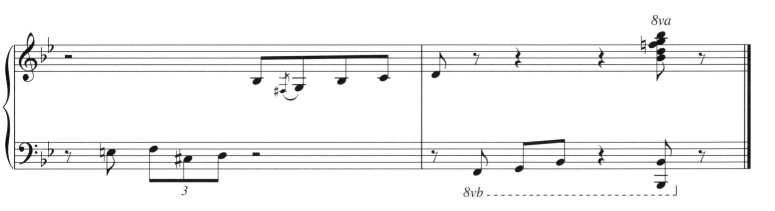

SHAKE ME I RATTLE
(Squeeze Me I Cry)

Words and Music by HAL HACKADY
and CHARLES NAYLOR

Moderately Slow and Smoothly

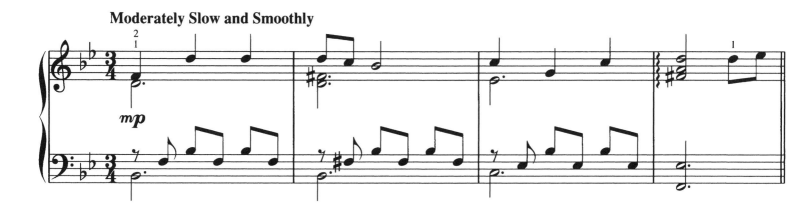

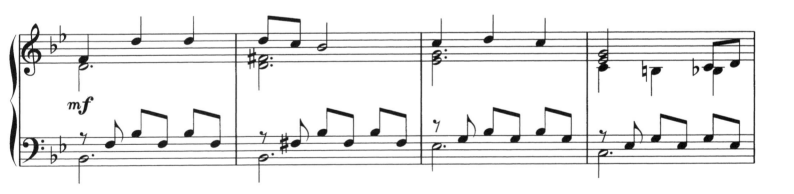

72

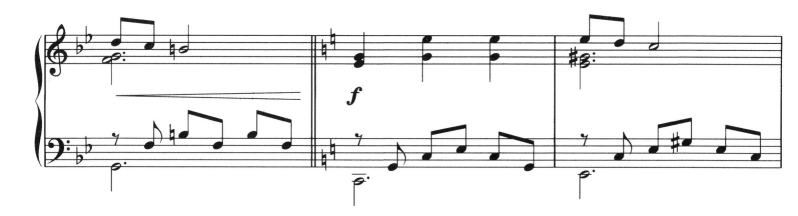

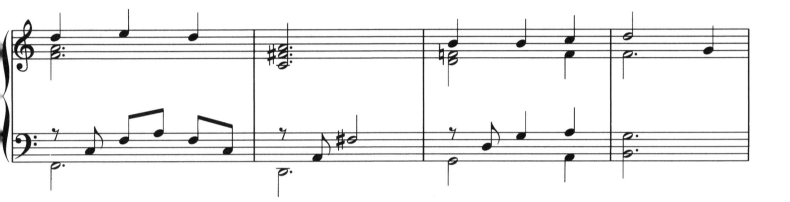

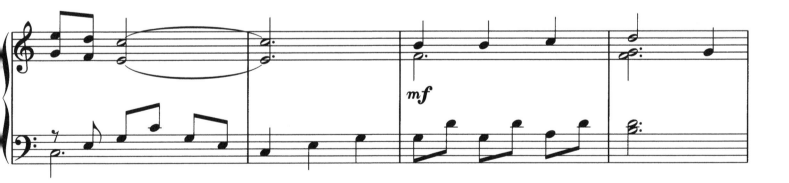

SOMEWHERE IN MY MEMORY

from the Twentieth Century Fox Motion Picture HOME ALONE

Words by LESLIE BRICUSSE
Music by JOHN WILLIAMS

Gently and with simplicity

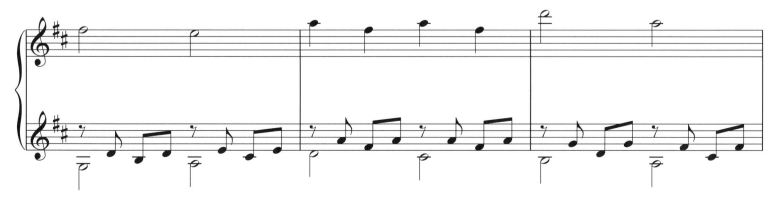

THE STAR CAROL

Lyric by WIHLA HUTSON
Music by ALFRED BURT

Tenderly, with much expression

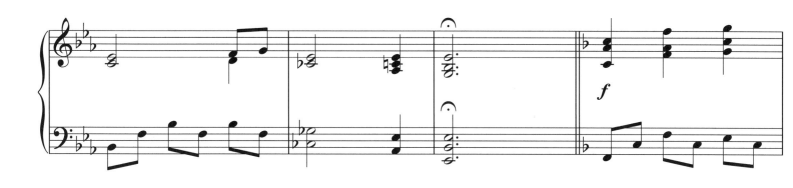

rit.

SUZY SNOWFLAKE

Words and Music by SID TEPPER
and ROY BENNETT

Moderately

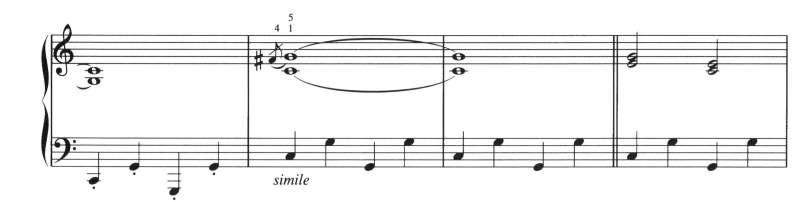

simile

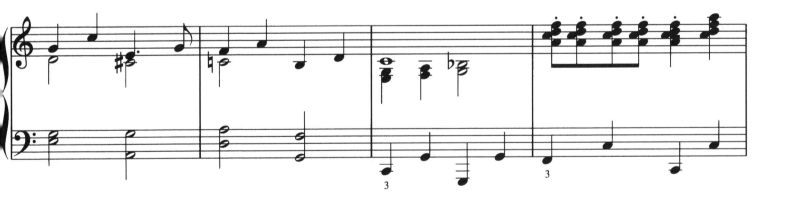

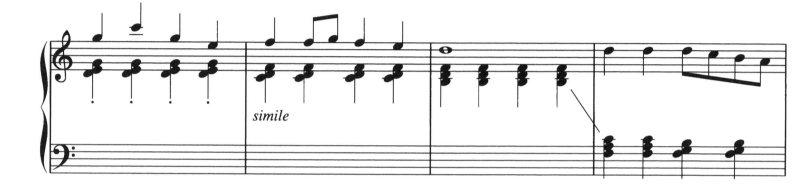

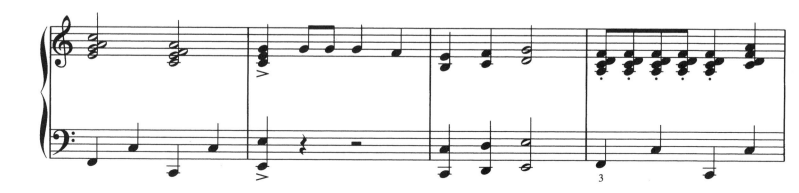

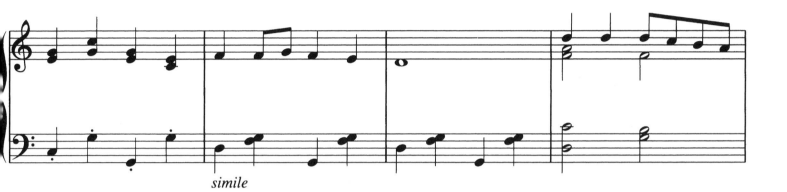

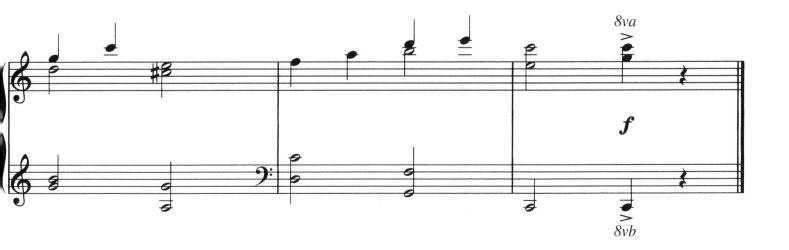

YOUR FAVORITE MUSIC

ARRANGED FOR PIANO SOLO

The Classical Wedding
Over 40 piano solos perfect for any wedding: Air on the G String • Bridal Chorus • Canon in D • Eine kleine Nachtmusik • Jesu, Joy of Man's Desiring • O Mio Babbino Caro • Rondeau • Sheep May Safely Graze • Trumpet Voluntary • Wedding March • and more.
00220029 ....$12.95

Disney Piano Solos
Features 14 Disney hits: Be Our Guest • Can You Feel the Love Tonight • Chim Chim Cher-ee • Go the Distance • Hakuna Matata • Kiss the Girl • Part of Your World • Reflection • Someday • A Whole New World • Zip-A-Dee-Doo-Dah • and more.
00313128 ....$12.95

Great Classical Themes
67 selections from works for symphony orchestra, chamber music, oratorio and art song. Includes: Canon in D (Pachelbel) • Piano Concerto in A Minor (Schumann) • Prelude to the Afternoon of a Faun (Debussy) • Symphony No. 5 in C Minor (Beethoven) • more.
00310300 ....$14.95

I Could Sing of Your Love Forever
15 sacred songs: Awesome God • The Heart of Worship • I Could Sing of Your Love Forever • Knowing You • Let My Words Be Few • My Utmost for His Highest • Open the Eyes of My Heart • The Potter's Hand • Shout to the North • There Is a Redeemer • and more.
00310905 ....$12.95

Best of Billy Joel
Features solo piano arrangements of 19 huge hits from this pop superstar: Allentown • Honesty • It's Still Rock and Roll to Me • Just the Way You Are • Keeping the Faith • The Longest Time • Only the Good Die Young • Piano Man • She's Always a Woman • Tell Her About It • Uptown Girl • We Didn't Start the Fire • and more.
00306389 ....$12.95

Elton John Collection
22 songs from this pop piano master, including: Bennie and the Jets • Can You Feel the Love Tonight • Candle in the Wind • Daniel • I Guess That's Why They Call It the Blues • Rocket Man • Sacrifice • Your Song • and more.
00306040 ....$12.95

Andrew Lloyd Webber
14 pieces, including: All I Ask of You • Don't Cry for Me Argentina • Memory • The Music of the Night • Phantom of the Opera • Pie Jesu • and more.

00292001 ....$14.95

The Man from Snowy River
6 piano solo selections, including: Jessica's Theme (Breaking In the Colt) • Main Title Theme • Now Do We Fight Then (Taming the Stallion) • and more.

00313076 ....$10.99

The Phantom of the Opera
9 songs from the beloved Andrew Lloyd Webber musical, including: All I Ask of You • Angel of Music • Masquerade • The Music of the Night • The Phantom of the Opera • The Point of No Return • Prima Donna • Think of Me • Wishing You Were Somehow Here Again.
00292005 ....$15.99

Piano Solos for All Occasions
This complete resource for every pianist includes delightful solo arrangements of 65 songs: Ain't Misbehavin' • Ave Maria • Bridal Chorus • Canon in D • Edelweiss • Für Elise • Georgia on My Mind • The Girl from Ipanema • The Godfather • Memory • Misty • Moon River • My Heart Will Go On • Route 66 • Stella by Starlight • When I Fall in Love • and scores more.
00310964 ....$19.95

Pirates of the Caribbean – The Curse of the Black Pearl
8 selections from Klaus Badelt's brilliant score: The Black Pearl • Blood Ritual/Moonlight Serenade • He's a Pirate • The Medallion Calls • One Last Shot • To the Pirates' Cave! • Underwater March. Includes photos from the film.
00313256 ....$17.95

Shout to the Lord
Moving arrangements of 14 praise favorites as interpreted by Phillip Keveren: As the Deer • El Shaddai • How Beautiful • How Majestic Is Your Name • More Precious Than Silver • Oh Lord, You're Beautiful • Shine, Jesus, Shine • Shout to the Lord • and more.
00310699 ....$12.95

Michael W. Smith – Freedom
All 12 tunes from the first instrumental CD by this multi-million-selling CCM artist: The Call • Carol Ann • Cry of the Heart • Free Man • Freedom • Freedom Battle • The Giving • Hibernia • Letter to Sarah • The Offering • Prayer for Taylor • Thy Word.
00306460 ....$16.95

Smooth Jazz
13 contemporary jazz favorites, including: Cast Your Fate to the Wind • Feels So Good • Home • Just the Two of Us • Morning Dance • Mountain Dance • Peg • She Could Be Mine • Silhouette • Songbird • This Masquerade • Turn Your Love Around • We're in This Love Together.
00311158 ....$12.95

Ultimate New Age
A great collection of 37 contemporary instrumental pieces. Includes: Angel's Flight • Barcelona • Celestial Soda Pop • Chariots of Fire • Cristofori's Dream • A Day Without Rain • First Kiss • Gone • Lullaby • The Memory of Trees • Return to the Heart • The Steamroller • Tubular Bells • The Velocity of Love • Watermark • more.
00311160 ....$17.95

The Best of Yanni
Solo arrangements of 11 songs: Almost a Whisper • First Touch • Marching Season • The Mermaid • Nostalgia • The Rain Must Fall • Reflections of Passion • Secret Vows • Swept Away • True Nature • A Word in Private.
00308145 ....$16.95

FOR MORE INFORMATION, SEE YOUR LOCAL MUSIC DEALER,
OR WRITE TO:

HAL•LEONARD® CORPORATION
7777 W. BLUEMOUND RD. P.O. BOX 13819 MILWAUKEE, WI 53213

Visit Hal Leonard online at www.halleonard.com

Prices, contents, and availability subject to change without notice.
Disney characters and artwork © Disney Enterprises, Inc.

0409

Christmas Collections
from Hal Leonard
All books arranged for piano, voice & guitar.

All-Time Christmas Favorites – Second Edition
This second edition features an all-star lineup of 32 Christmas classics, including: Blue Christmas • The Chipmunk Song • The Christmas Song • Frosty the Snow Man • Here Comes Santa Claus • I Saw Mommy Kissing Santa Claus • Jingle-Bell Rock • Let It Snow! Let It Snow! Let It Snow! • Merry Christmas, Darling • Nuttin' for Christmas • Rockin' Around the Christmas Tree • Rudolph the Red-Nosed Reindeer • Santa, Bring My Baby Back (To Me) • There Is No Christmas like a Home Christmas • and more.
00359051...$14.99

The Best Christmas Songs Ever – 4th Edition
69 all-time favorites are included in the 4th edition of this collection of Christmas tunes. Includes: Auld Lang Syne • Coventry Carol • Frosty the Snow Man • Happy Holiday • It Came Upon the Midnight Clear • O Holy Night • Rudolph the Red-Nosed Reindeer • Silver Bells • What Child Is This? • and many more.
00359130...$21.99

The Big Book of Christmas Songs – 2nd Edition
An outstanding collection of over 120 all-time Christmas favorites and hard-to-find classics. Features: Angels We Have Heard on High • As Each Happy Christmas • Auld Lang Syne • The Boar's Head Carol • Christ Was Born on Christmas Day • Bring a Torch Jeannette, Isabella • Carol of the Bells • Coventry Carol • Deck the Halls • The First Noel • The Friendly Beasts • God Rest Ye Merry Gentlemen • I Heard the Bells on Christmas Day • It Came Upon a Midnight Clear • Jesu, Joy of Man's Desiring • Joy to the World • Masters in This Hall • O Holy Night • The Story of the Shepherd • 'Twas the Night Before Christmas • What Child Is This? • and many more. Includes guitar chord frames.
00311520...$19.95

Christmas Songs – Budget Books
Save some money this Christmas with this fabulous budget-priced collection of 100 holiday favorites: All I Want for Christmas Is You • Christmas Time Is Here • Feliz Navidad • Grandma Got Run Over by a Reindeer • Happy Holiday • I'll Be Home for Christmas • Jesus Born on This Day • Last Christmas • Merry Christmas, Baby • O Holy Night • Please Come Home for Christmas • Rockin' Around the Christmas Tree • Some Children See Him • We Need a Little Christmas • What Child Is This? • and more.
00310887...$12.99

The Definitive Christmas Collection – 3rd Edition
Revised with even more Christmas classics, this must-have 3rd edition contains 127 top songs, such as: Blue Christmas • Christmas Time Is Here • Do You Hear What I Hear • The First Noel • A Holly Jolly Christmas • Jingle-Bell Rock • Little Saint Nick • Merry Christmas, Darling • O Holy Night • Rudolph, the Red-Nosed Reindeer • Silver and Gold • We Need a Little Christmas • You're All I Want for Christmas • and more!
00311602...$24.95

Essential Songs – Christmas
Over 100 essential holiday favorites: Blue Christmas • The Christmas Song • Deck the Hall • Frosty the Snow Man • A Holly Jolly Christmas • I'll Be Home for Christmas • Joy to the World • Let It Snow! Let It Snow! Let It Snow! • My Favorite Things • Rudolph the Red-Nosed Reindeer • Silver Bells • and more!
00311241...$24.95

Happy Holidays
50 favorite songs of the holiday season, including: Baby, It's Cold Outside • The Christmas Shoes • Emmanuel • The First Chanukah Night • The Gift • Happy Holiday • I Yust Go Nuts at Christmas • The Most Wonderful Time of the Year • Silver Bells • Who Would Imagine a King • Wonderful Christmastime • and more.
00310909...$17.95

Tim Burton's The Nightmare Before Christmas
This book features 11 songs from Tim Burton's creepy animated classic, with music and lyrics by Danny Elfman. Songs include: Jack's Lament • Jack's Obsession • Kidnap the Sandy Claws • Making Christmas • Oogie Boogie's Song • Poor Jack • Sally's Song • This Is Halloween • Town Meeting Song • What's This? • Finale/Reprise.
00312488...$12.99

Ultimate Christmas – 3rd Edition
100 seasonal favorites: Auld Lang Syne • Bring a Torch, Jeannette, Isabella • Carol of the Bells • The Chipmunk Song • Christmas Time Is Here • The First Noel • Frosty the Snow Man • Gesù Bambino • Happy Holiday • Happy Xmas (War Is Over) • Hymne • Jesu, Joy of Man's Desiring • Jingle-Bell Rock • March of the Toys • My Favorite Things • The Night Before Christmas Song • Pretty Paper • Silver and Gold • Silver Bells • Suzy Snowflake • What Child Is This • The Wonderful World of Christmas • and more.
00361399 ....$19.95

THE ULTIMATE SONGBOOKS

HAL•LEONARD

PIANO PLAY-ALONG

These great songbook/CD packs come with our standard arrangements for piano and voice with guitar chord frames plus a CD.

The CD includes a full performance of each song, as well as a second track without the piano part so you can play "lead" with the band!

1. Movie Music
00311072 P/V/G $14.95

2. Jazz Ballads
00311073 P/V/G $14.95

3. Timeless Pop
00311074 P/V/G $14.99

4. Broadway Classics
00311075 P/V/G $14.95

5. Disney
00311076 P/V/G $14.95

6. Country Standards
00311077 P/V/G $14.99

7. Love Songs
00311078 P/V/G $14.95

8. Classical Themes
00311079 Piano Solo $14.95

9. Children's Songs
0311080 P/V/G $14.95

10. Wedding Classics
00311081 Piano Solo $14.95

11. Wedding Favorites
00311097 P/V/G $14.95

12. Christmas Favorites
00311137 P/V/G $15.95

13. Yuletide Favorites
00311138 P/V/G $14.95

14. Pop Ballads
00311145 P/V/G $14.95

15. Favorite Standards
00311146 P/V/G $14.95

16. TV Classics
00311147 P/V/G $14.95

17. Movie Favorites
00311148 P/V/G $14.95

18. Jazz Standards
00311149 P/V/G $14.95

19. Contemporary Hits
00311162 P/V/G $14.95

20. R&B Ballads
00311163 P/V/G $14.95

21. Big Band
00311164 P/V/G $14.95

22. Rock Classics
00311165 P/V/G $14.95

23. Worship Classics
00311166 P/V/G $14.95

24. Les Misérables
00311169 P/V/G $14.95

25. The Sound of Music
00311175 P/V/G $15.99

26. Andrew Lloyd Webber Favorites
00311178 P/V/G $14.95

27. Andrew Lloyd Webber Greats
00311179 P/V/G $14.95

28. Lennon & McCartney
00311180 P/V/G $14.95

29. The Beach Boys
00311181 P/V/G $14.95

30. Elton John
00311182 P/V/G $14.95

31. Carpenters
00311183 P/V/G $14.95

32. Bacharach & David
00311218 P/V/G $14.95

33. Peanuts™
00311227 P/V/G $14.95

34. Charlie Brown Christmas
00311228 P/V/G $15.95

35. Elvis Presley Hits
00311230 P/V/G $14.95

36. Elvis Presley Greats
00311231 P/V/G $14.95

37. Contemporary Christian
00311232 P/V/G $14.95

38. Duke Ellington – Standards
00311233 P/V/G $14.95

39. Duke Ellington – Classics
00311234 P/V/G $14.95

40. Showtunes
00311237 P/V/G $14.95

41. Rodgers & Hammerstein
00311238 P/V/G $14.95

42. Irving Berlin
00311239 P/V/G $14.95

43. Jerome Kern
00311240 P/V/G $14.95

44. Frank Sinatra – Popular Hits
00311277 P/V/G $14.95

45. Frank Sinatra – Most Requested Songs
00311278 P/V/G $14.95

46. Wicked
00311317 P/V/G $15.99

47. Rent
00311319 P/V/G $14.95

48. Christmas Carols
00311332 P/V/G $14.95

49. Holiday Hits
00311333 P/V/G $15.99

50. Disney Classics
00311417 P/V/G $14.95

51. High School Musical
00311421 P/V/G $19.95

52. Andrew Lloyd Webber Classics
00311422 P/V/G $14.95

53. Grease
00311450 P/V/G $14.95

54. Broadway Favorites
00311451 P/V/G $14.95

55. The 1940s
00311453 P/V/G $14.95

56. The 1950s
00311459 P/V/G $14.95

57. The 1960s
00311460 P/V/G $14.99

58. The 1970s
00311461 P/V/G $14.99

59. The 1980s
00311462 P/V/G $14.99

60. The 1990s
00311463 P/V/G $14.99

61. Billy Joel Favorites
00311464 P/V/G $14.95

62. Billy Joel Hits
00311465 P/V/G $14.95

63. High School Musical 2
00311470 P/V/G $19.95

64. God Bless America
00311489 P/V/G $14.95

65. Casting Crowns
00311494 P/V/G $14.95

66. Hannah Montana
00311772 P/V/G $19.95

67. Broadway Gems
00311803 P/V/G $14.99

68. Lennon & McCartney Favorites
00311804 P/V/G $14.99

69. Pirates of the Caribbean
00311807 P/V/G $14.95

70. "Tomorrow," "Put on a Happy Face," And Other Charles Strouse Hits
00311821 P/V/G $14.99

71. Rock Band
00311822 P/V/G $14.99

72. High School Musical 3
00311826 P/V/G $19.99

73. Mamma Mia! – The Movie
00311831 P/V/G $14.99

74. Cole Porter
00311844 P/V/G $14.99

75. Twilight
00311860 P/V/G $16.99

76. Pride & Prejudice
00311862 P/V/G $14.99

77. Elton John Favorites
00311884 P/V/G $14.99

78. Eric Clapton
00311885 P/V/G $14.99

79. Tangos
00311886 P/V/G $14.99

80. Fiddler on the Roof
00311887 P/V/G $14.99

81. Josh Groban
00311901 P/V/G $14.99

82. Lionel Richie
00311902 P/V/G $14.99

83. Phantom of the Opera
00311903 P/V/G $14.99

84. Antonio Carlos Jobim Favorites
00311919 P/V/G $14.99

85. Latin Favorites
00311920 P/V/G $14.99

87. Patsy Cline
00311936 P/V/G $14.99

88. Neil Diamond
00311937 P/V/G $14.99

89. Favorite Hymns
00311940 P/V/G $14.99

90. Irish Favorites
00311969 P/V/G $14.99

91. Broadway Jazz
00311972 P/V/G $14.99

92. Disney Favorites
00311973 P/V/G $14.99

93. The Twilight Saga: New Moon – Soundtrack
00311974 P/V/G $16.99

94. The Twilight Saga: New Moon – Score
00311975 P/V/G $16.99

95. Taylor Swift
00311984 P/V/G $14.99

96. Best of Lennon & McCartney
00311996 P/V/G $14.99

FOR MORE INFORMATION, SEE YOUR LOCAL MUSIC DEALER, OR WRITE TO:

HAL•LEONARD® CORPORATION
7777 W. BLUEMOUND RD. P.O. BOX 13819 MILWAUKEE, WI 53213

Visit Hal Leonard Online at **www.halleonard.com**

Prices, contents, and availability subject to change without notice.
Disney characters and artwork © Disney Enterprises, Inc.

0810